Vice President

Julie Murray

Abdo
MY GOVERNMENT
Kids

abdopublishing.com

Published by Abdo Kids, a division of ABDO, PO Box 398166, Minneapolis, Minnesota 55439.
Copyright © 2018 by Abdo Consulting Group, Inc. International copyrights reserved in all countries.
No part of this book may be reproduced in any form without written permission from the publisher.

Printed in the United States of America, North Mankato, Minnesota.

102017

012018

 THIS BOOK CONTAINS
RECYCLED MATERIALS

Photo Credits: Alamy, AP Images, Getty Images, iStock, Shutterstock,
©US White House p.15,22, ©US Navy p.22, ©US Congress p.23

Production Contributors: Teddy Borth, Jennie Forsberg, Grace Hansen

Design Contributors: Christina Doffing, Candice Keimig, Dorothy Toth

Publisher's Cataloging in Publication Data

Names: Murray, Julie, author.

Title: Vice President / by Julie Murray.

Description: Minneapolis, Minnesota : Abdo Kids, 2018. | Series: My government |
    Includes glossary, index and online resource (page 24).

Identifiers: LCCN 2017908177 | ISBN 9781532104022 (lib.bdg.) | ISBN 9781532105142 (ebook) |
    ISBN 9781532105708 (Read-to-me ebook)

Subjects: LCSH: Vice Presidents--United States--Juvenile literature. | United States--History--Juvenile
    literature.

Classification: DDC 352.230973--dc23

LC record available at https://lccn.loc.gov/2017908177

Table of Contents

Vice President 4

What is the
VP's Job? 22

Glossary 23

Index 24

Abdo Kids Code 24

Vice President

Someone runs for president.

It happens every 4 years.

They choose a VP.

The VP had to be born in the USA. They must be at least 35.

7

People choose who they want.

They vote. One team wins!

John Adams was a VP. He was the first!

The VP has a big job to do!

They help the president.

15

They lead the **Senate**.

They help pass laws. They can break a tie vote.

Chloe meets the VP.

What is the VP's Job?

2nd in charge

Help pass laws

Help the president

Lead the Senate

Glossary

law
the system of rules a country or community recognizes.

Senate
a group that is a part of the United States Congress and helps run the country.

Index

Adams, John 10

laws 18

president 4, 14

responsibilities 12, 14, 16, 18

rules 6

Senate 16, 18

vote 8

Abdo Kids ONLINE
FREE! ONLINE MULTIMEDIA RESOURCES

Visit **abdokids.com** and use this code to access crafts, games, videos, and more!

Abdo Kids Code:
MVK4022